KNOW YOUR NUMBER

How to turn business success into lasting financial freedom

November 2018
Dear Scott + Dani,
Helping great people like you
is why I love what I do.
Thanks for being wonderful
clients and friends. See you in 2019!.

Love,
Bill

KNOW YOUR NUMBER

*How to turn business success
into lasting financial freedom*

Bill Hammer, Jr.
Certified Financial Planner™

Visit us online at www.hammerwealthgroup.com.

ISBN: 978-0-692-14084-0

Cover design by Adam Renvoize
Interior design by Alan Barnett

This book is for my incredible wife, Emma.
A dozen years later, I feel like we're just getting started.

TABLE OF CONTENTS

3   Warning: This Book Isn't for Everybody

11   **PART 1: Creating Your Plan**

13   How Successful Exits Can Disappear

17   What's Your Vision?

21   What's Your Number?

29   What's Your Plan?

37   Two Planning Case Studies

51   **PART 2: Working Your Plan**

53   Before You Invest a Dollar, Do This

59   The Greatest Risk to Preserving Your Wealth

65   How to Earn Real-Life Returns

71   How to Stay Disciplined for Decades

77   How to Find Your Coach

83   What a Freedom Portfolio Looks Like

89   How to Make Volatility Meaningless

93   How to Invest Your Multiplier Bucket Like a Boss

97   3 Simple Things You Can Do Next

"It requires a great deal of boldness and a great deal of caution to make a great fortune; and when you have got it, it requires ten times as much wit to keep it."

—*Victor Rothschild*

WARNING: This Book Isn't for Everybody

> **❝** An entrepreneur is someone who jumps off a cliff and builds a plane on the way down. **❞**
>
> —*Reid Hoffman, founder of LinkedIn*

In case you forgot, let me remind you—you're not normal.

You're an entrepreneur, so you eat risk for breakfast. You chase opportunity where others are running from danger. You see problems and build businesses that solve those problems.

And you play a totally different financial game than everyone else.

You are paid for results, not time or effort. You get more upside because you accept more financial risk. Your most valuable asset is your business, not a 401(k).

Bottom line, you have more power to shape your financial future than most people do. And that's why entrepreneurs create wealth like no other group.

The Forbes 400 list is full of entrepreneurs (Jeff Bezos, Bill Gates, Elon Musk, etc.) or children of entrepreneurs (Sam Walton's kids).

So normal financial advice for people with normal jobs living normal lives won't cut it for you. Budgets, coupons, skipping Starbucks, and other scarcity-minded nonsense won't get you where you want to go.

That's why I wrote this book for serious entrepreneurs who have built highly successful businesses. This book is for those of you who already have something to lose if you're not careful.

Bit by bit, step by step, little by little, you've built a company.

You were tough enough, smart enough, and persistent enough to get where you are today. And your business survived some near-death experiences along the way.

You've already turned **nothing** into **something,** and **something** into **something valuable.** Now you have the rare opportunity to do what most people only dream about—to turn **a valuable asset you built** into **lasting financial freedom.**

Just like every other worthwhile goal you've accomplished, achieving financial freedom starts with asking the right questions. Unfortunately, most entrepreneurs are so focused on their business's financial health they don't give their personal money the attention it deserves. That leads to asking bad questions like:

What should I do with my money?

That question might lead you to put some money here, invest some money there, or maybe hand it over to people you hope know what they're doing—not exactly a recipe for success.

But ask a better question—one that's focused on the *outcome* you want to achieve—and you'll get a better answer. For example:

How will I use money to create freedom in my life?

That question will spark a much more interesting, helpful answer. When you're clear on what you want to accomplish, figuring out the steps you need to take becomes much easier.

Managing your money can be made to appear immensely complicated and confusing.

Complexity kills execution, so here we're going to simplify. If you read no further, know this—there are only two financial outcomes for your life:

1. **Your money runs out someday.** You're fine for a while, but the well eventually runs dry or you're forced to cut expenses to the bone.

2. **You create lasting financial freedom.** That's what this book is about.

What exactly is lasting financial freedom (LFF)?

Lasting financial freedom (we'll call it LFF for short) is having plenty of income whether you work or not for as long as you live.

It's not a financial goal. It's *the* financial goal.

It doesn't mean you *won't* ever earn another penny—it just means you *won't have to* earn another penny. Big difference.

When you started out, someone else's business paid you for your work. Then your own business paid you for your work. The final frontier is when your personal assets keep paying you no matter what you do.

Some people call this "f-you money," but I think of it as *free you* money.

LFF is a river that replenishes itself even as you draw water from it over decades (if not generations).

Properly cared for, it can generate *surplus* water you can generously share with family, friends, and causes you believe in.

LFF isn't about material things like Ferraris, mansions, or private jets. Sure, if getting your dream car is important to you it can help, but LFF is *really* about creating freedom.

And isn't that why you chose the entrepreneurial path in the first place?

You love the freedom to run the business your way, hire the talent you want, and come and go as you please—wearing whatever you want! But over time, you'd also like to enjoy the freedom that comes from knowing your family's financial future is permanently secure.

The freedom to spend more time with the people you care about most…

The freedom to make an even bigger dent in the universe—at home, in business, or for causes that matter to you…

The freedom to keep building businesses around what you're really good at…

The freedom to travel and slow your pace to a jog whenever you'd like.

But most of all, you want to enjoy freedom that *lasts*. And lasting financial freedom has three distinct characteristics.

1. LFF is about how *free* you are, not how rich you are

Cornelius Vanderbilt left a $100 million estate when he died in 1877.[1] It was more money than was in the U.S. Treasury at the time.

For context, $100 million in 1877 was like $100 *billion* or more today—more than enough to sustain his family for generations.

Yet within 50 years, one of his descendants died penniless. In fact, there was not a single millionaire at a 1973 Vanderbilt family reunion of 120 descendants. How is that possible?

The problem wasn't the amount Vanderbilt left. The problem was his heirs' spending, which required a few hundred million more in principal.

You see, LFF isn't about an absolute number of dollars. It's about how easily your assets can generate the income you need to fund your lifestyle.

Imagine three entrepreneurs—Unicorn Eugene, High-Roller Henry, and Liquid Laura.

Unicorn Eugene draws just enough salary to live modestly from his $50 million private business that's growing like crazy. Every spare dollar gets reinvested back into the business.

High-Roller Henry's business generates $1 million of personal income a year, but Henry spends all of it. His business isn't worth much to a buyer, and he's saved little over the years.

Liquid Laura owns a small, profitable business and lives on $250,000 a year. She's built up personal assets that will kick out $300,000 a year in income when she turns on the faucet.

Eugene and Henry may have a higher net worth, but Laura's lifestyle wouldn't change a bit if she woke up tomorrow and shut down her business.

So…who's got the freedom?

2. LFF has a price tag

Recently, one of my clients showed me exactly how he planned to grow his business from 50 locations to 100 in the next few years.

His plan was clear and simple because everything was weighed against his goal of 100 locations.

If a decision got him closer or sped up the timeline, it was a "yes." If not, it was a "no" or a "not now."

Why should your money be any different?

If you want to create LFF *as you define it,* you must know its price tag. Once you do, you'll be able to answer difficult questions like…

- When and how should I take some (or all) of my chips off the table?
- How much do I need to sell my business for in order to create LFF?
- Could I create LFF without selling my business? How soon?
- Could I afford to give up some equity to build a team that can run the business without me?

- Should I focus more on growing cash flow or equity value?
- How could I spend more time with family without torpedoing our lifestyle?

If you don't know your number, you can't answer these important questions. You can only guess. In the coming chapters, I'm going to help you figure it out with total certainty.

3. LFF is about disciplined behavior, not IQ

Creating LFF is driven by what *you* do, not external factors you can't predict or control. If you are hostage to financial news or "the market," you're doing it wrong.

Think of the fittest person you know around your age. Why is she in better shape than you?

It's not because she's smarter. And she doesn't live near better grocery stores, gyms, or personal trainers.

So what's the difference? Disciplined, consistent behavior.

She's kept good habits for years. Slowly and steadily, those daily habits added up.

Creating financial freedom works the same way. You need to get in shape and then stay in shape for a lifetime.

What you *think* about doing with your money is worthless. What you actually *do* is worth something. What you do consistently over decades is priceless.

And no matter how much technology changes our lives, human nature continually finds ways to keep us from doing what we know we should do.

You already have all the IQ points you'll need if you've built a successful company (or two, or ten).

The only question is whether you'll take the necessary steps to secure LFF.

This book is divided into two parts that will show you how.

In Part 1, I'll take you through a series of short exercises designed to give you total clarity on your LFF Number and the specific action steps you can start taking to ensure you reach it.

In Part 2, I'll dive deeper into the tactical financial strategies that will help you execute your plan and make sure financial freedom lasts for the rest of your life.

So...
why should you bother listening to me?

I know what makes successful entrepreneurs tick because I work with them every day.

More importantly, *I'm an entrepreneur, too.* I've lived the roller-coaster and know how it feels.

I've had three years' worth of bad breaks in one quarter. I've liquidated retirement accounts or run up credit cards to survive. I've had holidays ruined by emails bearing bad news.

But I wouldn't have it any other way—because freedom matters as much to me as it does to you.

That's why I don't work for a big, fancy Wall Street firm that would tell me who I can and cannot work with, what product I need to push this month, what to wear, and how I should spend my time.

Instead, I built a business around doing what I love—helping serious entrepreneurs turn business success into lasting financial freedom.

Professionally, I'm a Certified Financial Planner™. I've written another book besides this one (*The 7 Secrets of Extraordinary Investors*), and I've been quoted in media like *The Wall Street Journal, CNBC, Financial Advisor Magazine,* and *Kiplinger.*

I'm serious about my craft. But in my heart, I'm an entrepreneur who absolutely loves business.

That's why it's a blast having clients who run all kinds of companies—real estate, professional services, healthcare, staffing, consulting, software, design, franchising, and construction, just to name a few.

Most of my clients' businesses do between $5 million and $50 million, though some are in the "billionaire-in-training" program.

No matter their net worth, they all have one thing in common— their plates are always full. The stakes keep getting higher, the puzzle pieces keep multiplying, yet their free time keeps shrinking.

That's a recipe for bigger, more expensive mistakes. They can't do it all and certainly don't want to do it all, so they hire me to help.

My 3 promises to you

I'm not a theorist or an academic. I spend my time in the financial trenches helping real business owners with real families and real money.

This book is based on what I've learned from experience—the no-brainer decisions you should copy, the meaningless details you should ignore, and the money-sucking mistakes you must avoid.

It's short because you don't have the time or desire to read an encyclopedia on this stuff. You want actionable ideas, not a lecture. (Have you ever wished that a book was longer? I sure haven't.)

Most of all, I promise you three things:

1. A step-by-step process for making better financial decisions.

2. A conversational book without the technical jargon.

3. Actionable advice you can actually use.

Sound good? Let's get started.

PART 1

BUILDING YOUR PLAN

In Part 1, I'm going to show you how to think about creating LFF. You'll learn how to get clear on what financial freedom means to you, put a price and deadline on it, find a compelling purpose to motivate you, and craft a plan for getting there.

The exercises don't take very long to complete, so they should give you a very high return on invested time (ROIT).

How Successful Exits Can Disappear

"It is remarkable how much long-term advantage people like us have gotten by trying to be consistently not stupid instead of trying to be very intelligent."

—Charlie Munger,
Warren Buffett's business partner of 50+ years

If you own a valuable company, you might think, *"All I need to do is sell my company for a big number, and then I'm set."*

The truth is, that rarely happens. All too often, entrepreneurs achieve major financial success—huge incomes, big exits, etc.—only to find it doesn't stick. You can probably think of one person you know right now who squandered big-time financial success.

If you're not careful, the financial rewards from building a serious company over a decade or more can slip away in a few years.

Here's how that happens.

Meet Adam

Adam (real client, fake name) is a brilliant serial entrepreneur who starts businesses, grows them, and then sells them. In fact, he called me because he was about to sell one of his companies for a multi-million dollar payday.

I'll never forget what he said within the first five minutes:

> *"I had a big exit, and I blew it. I don't want*
> *to make the same mistakes again."*

Adam told me he bootstrapped a simple, unsexy services business in his late 20s and sold it in his early 30s to a massive strategic buyer.

He walked away with about *$15 million after taxes* between upfront cash and his earn-out.

It had been 10 years since Adam's big exit, but only $3 million was left.

Where did the other $12 million go?

Divorce? Nope, he's been happily married for over 20 years.

Mansions? Lovely house, but nothing extravagant.

Sports cars? I saw a Honda minivan in his driveway.

He avoided many of the easy traps. But he made several bad decisions that added up much quicker than he'd ever thought possible.

Post-exit, he believed everything he touched would turn to gold. This is common in young entrepreneurs who sell an early business for a lot of money. But the opportunity-seeking impulse that made him a great entrepreneur actually hurt him as an investor.

There were bad investments made with bad people who ended up in jail, and bad investments made with *good* people. There were overseas business ventures that completely blew up.

There were panicked decisions made near the bottom of the 2008 financial crisis, when he switched stocks with bonds just as the markets rocketed back up.

The worst part about these bad decisions is they were all rooted in one big mistake.

Adam had no plan **for his money. And money without a plan wanders off and gets lost.**

He had plans for his *company,* but no plan for the *money he made from that company.* Sound familiar?

He made random, disconnected decisions that weren't tied to a freedom-driven plan, just like every other entrepreneur who has blown millions.

We entrepreneurs believe we can do anything, and that's why we can build companies. But that doesn't mean we can do *everything.* The skills that have helped you make money in business may not help you keep that money or grow it into something lasting for your family.

Remember this—a plan turns financial freedom into *lasting* **financial freedom.**

And while a plan isn't a guarantee for success (there are bad plans, after all), *not having a plan* might as well be a guarantee for failure.

Why most financial "plans" aren't actually plans at all

Of course, in Adam's eyes he *did* have a plan. After all, one of his first post-exit decisions was to hire a money manager at a large, well-known financial firm.

You know, the kind who promises to help you outsmart the market, find the best managers, and predict what the economy will do next.

But all that really got Adam was a *portfolio,* not a plan or a process for protecting his financial freedom.

What he really needed was help clarifying what LFF looked like, figuring out exactly how much it would cost, and creating a plan to make that real.

Adam needed to make decisions that connected his *entire* financial picture—investing, asset protection, tax planning, estate planning—so his decisions would support, not threaten, LFF.

Entrepreneurs need comprehensive planning more than any group I know. Think of all the complexity, opportunity, and risk there is to manage:

Multiple legal entities, partnerships, real estate, industry disruption, tax law changes, legal threats, family changes—and on top of that you need to figure out how and when to monetize your ownership in a business.

Context is critical. Without a coherent, overarching plan, your decisions have none. How can any investment, insurance product, estate plan, or tax strategy make any sense outside of a big picture financial plan?

You won't create LFF from a cluttered financial garage full of disconnected parts you've collected over the years.

You'll create it when your financial parts create a powerful engine.

What's Your Vision?

"Greatness starts with a clear vision of the future.**"**

—*Simon Sinek,*
author of Start With Why

The first step to creating LFF isn't complicated. It all starts with answering a simple question:

What does financial freedom mean to me?

It's impossible to figure out what to do next until you know exactly what you want. How did you build your company? By creating a clear vision of what it looked like well before that vision became reality.

What if you wanted to 10× your business from $5 million to $50 million? You wouldn't start by just pouring more money into it; you would create a **vision** of what that $50 million business looks like. Then you would reverse engineer that vision into a series of steps.

Creating LFF starts the same way. Before you figure out what it will cost or the plan for making it real, you need to define what it looks like.

To make it as quick and easy as possible, all you have to do is list 5–10 things that need to be true in order for you to feel financially free. The following pages give you the space to do it right here in this book.

Start with what you want life to look like, and then we'll quantify that picture in dollars. These are life goals that just happen to cost money.

What has to be true for you to feel financially free? What are the criteria for you?

Do you want to travel the world until you figure out your next venture?

Where would you live? How would you spend your day?

Why is creating LFF so important to you and your family? What will you miss out on if you don't take serious action?

Start writing freely. Get into the flow. Your answers don't need to be complicated or completely final. They just need to be honest and personal. It's okay for Version 1.0 to be messy—you can always create Version 2.0 later and clean it up.

A few tips before you start writing

Eliminate distractions: Find a distraction-free zone (no kids, phone, laptops, etc.) where you can sip a drink you enjoy (coffee, wine, etc.). You need focused, creative time to think.

Write, don't type: Handwriting is slower, but it's better. You'll feel more creative and simultaneously internalize what you're writing. Typing makes you more likely to get writer's block.

Forget how for now: Don't start editing your ideas or getting stuck on details. Focus on creating the clearest picture of what LFF looks like for you. Planning and strategy come later.

Write in the present tense: Write as if everything is already true. Write with belief, not hope.

Look at the example answers below first: These will give you an idea of what your answers should look like.

Your LFF Vision
(Example Answers)

What must be true for you to feel financially free? Use as many or as few blanks as you need. Once you're done, put a star next to the most important items.

We can live like we do now without working. ✱

Our kitchen is totally renovated.

We are mortgage-free on our current home. ✱

We do four big trips a year (two domestic, two international). ✱

We give $25,000 a year to charities we love.

We can support our parents if they need help.

We can pay for four years of college tuition tomorrow if needed.

Why is creating LFF a must for you?

We worked hard and took too many risks to not see the payoff.

I'd be the first person in my family to create LFF.

So we can focus on living life, not making money.

If you don't take action, what might it cost you and your family?

We miss our "window of opportunity" to sell the company.

We get less quality time with the kids than they deserve.

We have to keep working like crazy to live our lifestyle.

Your LFF Vision

What must be true for you to feel financially free? Use as many or as few blanks as you need. Once you're done, put a star next to the most important items.

_____

_____

_____

_____

_____

_____

_____

Why is creating LFF a must for you?

_____

_____

_____

_____

If you don't take action, what might it cost you and your family?

_____

_____

_____

_____

What's Your Number?

> **"** People with clear, written goals, accomplish more in a shorter period of time than people without them could ever imagine. **"**

—*Brian Tracy,*
author of 70 books, including
The Psychology of Achievement

Defining what financial freedom means to you is a great first step, but you'll never get there until you know what that vision is going to cost.

If you were building a custom home, you wouldn't just give your wish list to your contractor. You'd want to know what building that vision was going to cost before you ever broke ground so you could plan accordingly.

Your LFF Vision is a financial hope. Once we put a cost to that vision, you'll have a financial **goal**. And for something to qualify as a financial goal, you need to answer the following:

How much, by when?

"Being financially free someday" is a hope.

Having $8,000,000 in investments within 10 years so you never need to work again…that's a goal.

In this chapter, you'll use the LFF Number Sheet to figure out your number and the date by which you want to reach it. All you have to do to fill it out is follow these six easy steps. At the end, you'll have a rock-solid goal in place.

Step 1: Estimate your cash and income needs

To get started, you'll need to determine approximately how much *income* and *cash* each item in your LFF Vision will require. Think of each like a separate bucket.

The *income* bucket holds the things you pay for **every year**—property taxes, phone, internet, utilities, mortgage, vacations, insurance, gym membership, food, fun, etc.

The *cash* bucket holds the things you pay for **once or temporarily**—college tuition, a wedding, home renovation, a car, a special experience, seed money for a future venture, etc.

If you're not sure what something costs, overestimate to be safe.

For example, let's say you still need to pay for your youngest child's undergraduate education. Estimate tuition for the most expensive option. If they get a scholarship or choose a cheaper school, great—you'll have more than enough cash to cover it.

If you're going to remodel your home, take the estimate you got from a contractor and add 50% or double it. Believe me.

If you're going to celebrate LFF with a trip around the world, take your best guess.

Don't get too bogged down with the cash bucket. It typically has the smallest impact on how large your LFF Number is since these are all "one and done" expenses.

Your current pre-tax income is a great starting point for estimating income needs, especially if your financial freedom lifestyle is pretty similar to your current lifestyle.

For example, if you live comfortably on $500,000 a year, then start there and adjust the number based on what you spend and save.

Let's say you make $500,000 and have been saving $100,000 a year in retirement accounts pre-tax. You probably live on $400,000 of pre-tax income.

Or maybe you plan to spend $35,000 a year more on travel once you're financially free. Then you'll add another $50,000 of pre-tax income to cover those trips, depending on your tax bracket and state income tax rate.

If you're struggling to figure out how much annual income you would need to live the lifestyle you want, start by thinking about monthly expenses.

When I ask people what they spend annually, they have no idea. But if I ask them what they spend *monthly*, they can ballpark that number pretty quickly.

Step 2: Convert your income needs into a lump sum

To create lasting financial freedom, you need to own investments that generate income. And, since living costs rise over time, your income will need to grow.

So—how much money will you need to live well and grow your income over time without depleting your resources?

There is an overwhelming amount of research on this topic, so I'll skip straight to the punch line: **4% or 25✕**.

For *every $1 million* of investment assets you have, you can draw *$40,000 a year* (4% before taxes) of income and make that money last…if you invest properly. You can't put it under a mattress or swing for the fences.

If your annual pre-tax income needs are $200,000 a year, then you'll need at least $5 million of invested assets ($200,000 × 25) to generate that income.

Do you want $30,000 a month of pre-tax income ($360,000/year)? Sock away $9 million (25 × $360,000), and you've created LFF.

And remember, the 25×/4% rule is the *maximum* you can draw and make your money last. If you have $10 million put away and only need $300,000 of pre-tax income (3%) or less, that provides even more cushion.

Here's a chart to help you figure out 25× or 4%:

Max Pre-tax Income per month	Max Pre-tax Income per year	Lump Sum Needed
$3,333/month	$40,000/year	$1,000,000
$16,666/month	$200,000/year	$5,000,000
$33,333/month	$400,000/year	$10,000,000
$83,333/month	$1,000,000/year	$25,000,000
$333,333/month	$2,000,000/year	$50,000,000

What if you already own some passive income investments (like real estate or a business) that send you checks? Just subtract that from your income needs.

Step 3: Add up your cash and income number

To find your total LFF Number, you add your cash and cash flow buckets together.

For example, let's say your cash bucket needs around $1 million for tuition, home remodels, and some seed money you want set aside for a future business.

Then, you settle on $30,000 a month in pre-tax income ($360,000 annually). That requires a $9 million income bucket ($360,000 × 25).

In that case, your LFF Number would be $10 million ($1 million cash bucket + $9 million income bucket).

Step 4: Pick a deadline

Knowing your number is great, but it's still not a goal until you pick a deadline. When must LFF happen by?

Is there a date in your mind? A milestone that is important to you (kids going to college, a birthday ending in a zero, etc.)?

What's the deadline that immediately popped into your head?

If you're struggling to pick one, pick a minimum date (everything goes perfectly) and a maximum date (takes longer but you're still happy with the timeline).

Step 5 (optional): Make adjustments

Once you know your LFF Number, you'll react one of three ways:

1. **Relief.** You are already there or almost there.

2. **Belief.** You aren't there yet, but you can see a clear, realistic path to that number.

3. **Disbelief.** Your number seems so impossible or far away you suddenly feel broke.

Disbelief means your number is too big, your deadline is too soon, or your business is too small.

If your number scares you, go back and redo it. Get rid of the "wants" and stick to the "needs." Focus on freedom, not stuff.

Or maybe your deadline is too soon. Move it back.

Or don't change a thing. Instead, start figuring out how to massively grow your business and/or reduce your current lifestyle so you can invest more.

LFF NUMBER SHEET

CASH

Item	Cost
College	$250,000
Remodel	$250,000
Future venture	$500,000
Total	$1,000,000

INCOME

Item	Income needed
Living	$260,000
Travel	$70,000
Other	$30,000
Annual income needs	$360,000

$$\times 25$$

Total	$9,000,000

Total cash	Total Income	LFF number
$1,000,000	+ $9,000,000 =	$10,000,000
		Deadline
		2024

LFF NUMBER SHEET

CASH

Item	Cost
Total	

INCOME

Item	Income needed
Annual income needs	

$\times$ **25**

Total	

Total cash		Total Income		LFF number
	+		=	
				Deadline

What's Your Plan?

❝ By failing to prepare,
you are preparing to fail. **❞**

—Benjamin Franklin,
one of America's most influential Founding Fathers

According to the Bureau of Labor Statistics, roughly 50% of businesses last five years. Even fewer that survive are profitable.

So if your business does millions of dollars in revenue each year, you're in rarified air. But that alone doesn't create financial freedom.

Earning a lot of money as an entrepreneur, famous professional athlete, or highly paid actor doesn't automatically turn into financial freedom. (Just ask Mike Tyson or Nicolas Cage.)

Still, many entrepreneurs think the financial freedom equation is this:

Great business = Financial freedom

Sure, building a great business increases your odds dramatically. But you need to figure out how to **turn your business success into financial freedom**.

You need to turn that equals sign into an arrow.

Successful business ⟶ **Financial freedom**

How do you do it? You build a bridge between the two—a plan.

Your biggest danger is your biggest opportunity

Have you ever worked too hard for too long, let your health backslide, spent little time with family, and burned out?

Have you ever swung the other way and focused so much on your family and health that your business started to suffer?

Of course. We all have.

Entrepreneurship is a balancing act. You make adjustments and find the right balance over time.

But you also need to find the right financial balance so you can grow your business while creating financial freedom for your family.

The single biggest financial opportunity and challenge entrepreneurs face is determining when to take chips off the table, how to take them off, how many to take off, and what to do with them once they're off.

Knowing your number provides context to answer that question, but a plan is what makes it happen.

What financial planning is and is not

Before we go on, I want you to understand what I mean by "financial planning."

Financial planning is **personal**. It's *your* plan, not your partner's plan, your sister's plan, or your spouse's plan. No two plans are the same.

Financial planning is **holistic**. You can't be all offense (saving, investing, growing a business) and no defense (insurance, asset protection, estate planning). Everything needs to be considered.

Financial planning is **life planning**. It isn't just about money. It's about making sure your financial decisions are perfectly aligned with how you want to live your life.

Financial planning is a **verb**. A plan isn't done once and put into a drawer. It's an ongoing process that evolves as you, your family, your business, your goals, and your priorities change.

Financial planning starts with **momentum**, not complexity. The simpler the first step, the easier it becomes to follow through. That's why I've designed a tool for you to use in this chapter that makes getting started as simple as possible.

The LFF 80/20 Planner

The LFF Planner™ is a simple matrix that helps you identify 80% of the key issues that will create or destroy your financial freedom in just a few minutes.

It's a quick way to discover the clear, actionable next steps you can take to make significant progress on creating financial freedom.

You'll do two of these—a **business plan and a personal plan**. Once you have both, you'll be able to identify where they are aligned or disconnected.

Each matrix will focus on **four key areas**:

➕ What must go right?

➖ What could go wrong?

❓ What questions need answers?

🙂 Who must get on or off the bus?

	Key results	Next steps
➕	What specific results must you achieve in order to hit your number on time?	What must you do in order to get those results?
➖	What could happen to prevent you from reaching (or delay achieving) your goal?	What can you do to stop this, or at least lower the odds of this happening?
❓	What questions must you find answers to in order to reach your goal?	Where can you find the answers?
☺	Who needs to get on or off the bus in order for you to reach your goal?	What must you do next?

Step 1: First plan business, then plan personal

I'm not saying the business plan is more important, but you'll find your business plan is easier to fill in. You've likely already thought through this area.

Step 2: Write your LFF Number and deadline at the top

Those two numbers need to be staring at you as you fill this in. They are your goal, so everything you write down needs to help you hit that dollar amount by that date.

Step 3: Identify "what" first (left side)

Do all four "results" boxes first. Clarify exactly what needs to happen, what could blow it, what needs to be answered, and the people you need to help you hit your dollar target and date.

Imagine you wake up the morning of your deadline and you've hit your number. Congratulations.

What **positive results** did your business produce to get there?

If your plan is to sell the business, start with the sale price you need to create financial freedom. Then back out the revenue, growth rates, margins, number of clients, or key numbers you need to get there.

If your plan is part sale and part cash flow, be specific.

Now imagine you missed your goal or hit it late.

What **negative results** caused you to fail?

What teammates or clients left? What weaknesses didn't get fixed? What could get you there, but way later than you want?

Nobody has all the answers, but we all have questions. Write down **critical questions** you need to answer but haven't yet. Maybe you need to set aside time, or maybe you haven't gone to the right source for the answer.

What tactics, strategies, facts, figures, or capabilities do you need to achieve your goal?

"Who" is on the bus solves a lot of "how to get there" problems.

Who is currently on the bus that needs to get off in order to get there on time? Who needs to get on the bus that isn't already on it?

Step 4: Figure out "how" (right side)

Now that you're clear on the key factors (left column), you can brainstorm ideas on how to create those results (right column).

For **positive results**, what are the key projects your team should focus on? What needs to be mapped out more clearly?

What do you need to keep doing, start doing, stop doing, do more, or do better?

Next, try to come up with solutions to those **negative results**.

How can you minimize that risk or totally eliminate it? What are some strategies you could use if that bad thing happened? Who has solved this problem before?

Once you've identified key **questions**, you need to figure out where to find answers. Don't just Google it; ask someone knowledgeable. Who already knows this stuff or can point you in the right direction?

You've identified **people** whom you need to hire or get rid of, but now you need to do something about it. Strategize your next steps.

Step 5: Repeat these steps for your personal plan

If you run a successful business, filling in the business plan is easy. You'll breeze through it.

But many serious entrepreneurs don't even know where to start on the personal side. It's the same process, but your personal financial picture isn't something you focus on much.

Here are a couple of tips if the personal side is raising your heart rate or making you sweat:

- It's okay to have a full ❓ and ☺ box but a lot of white space elsewhere. That just means you need a better team around you on the personal side (wealth advisor, accountant, attorney, etc.).

- Look at the examples in the coming chapters as a jump-off point for ideas. Then come back here and fill in your matrix.

- Set a timer, write what you can for five minutes (even if it's a mess), and then put it away for a while. Give your brain a chance to work subconsciously and come back to it later.

Step 6: Do an 80/20 analysis

You've heard of the Pareto Principle—80% of your results come from 20% of your actions. An 80/20 analysis should help you focus on the most important next steps.

Look at your two sheets and star or circle (ideally in a different color) the most crucial things you need to do next.

This will make it easier to come back to these lists and immediately take action.

Two Planning Case Studies

> ❝ I have not failed. I've just found 10,000 ways that won't work. ❞
>
> —*Thomas Edison,*
> *Inventor with over 1,000 registered patents*
> *and founder of 14 companies*
> *(including General Electric)*

Your business is probably the most valuable asset you own, so monetizing it somehow will play a significant role in creating your plan and hitting your number.

One very important thing you should keep in mind—**there's more than one way to monetize a business.**

Notice I said "monetizing" your business, not "selling" your business. Cashing out to a buyer may or may not be the best answer, depending on your business, personal goals, and family situation.

It's easy to view selling your business as the only way to monetize. Selling is sexier, strokes the ego, and allows you to walk away once the earn out is done.

But selling is not the best way to monetize for everyone, especially if you own a business worth a lot more in your hands than it is to a buyer.

Maybe you take some chips off the table in a funding round. Maybe you sell internally to partners. Or maybe you build a team that turns you into a passive owner over time.

There are so many options once you've built something valuable. Don't get stuck on just one—especially if it doesn't feel right for you.

The best way to understand the options, and how they fit into your plan, is to see them in action using real case studies.

These two are "inspired by" many of my entrepreneur clients. I've combined lots of client cases into two so that you can see some critical issues quickly.

These case studies will show you how planning works in real life, and help you do a second run through your own plan.

Case Study #1—Roy: Built to Sell

Roy is in his mid-40s, married, and has two teenage boys. He and his wife, Lydia, sat down with me because they have "no time or bandwidth to manage the personal picture" and "need accountability" to keep that picture in order.

FYI: Quotes indicate I'm using clients' actual words from my meeting notes.

Vision

After 15 years of building a software business from scratch, Roy and Lydia "want to live life without worrying about work." They'd love to travel more, possibly downsize from a house to an urban apartment, and rekindle their shared love of adventure.

That said, they "don't ever want to stop doing things or producing," and they "value experiences over material things." They want to show the boys how hard work pays off.

Financially, they "don't want the boys' education limited by money concerns." They want to teach their sons about money, investing, and financial responsibility.

Roy sees now as the right time to sell the business. The boys will be in college in five years and his industry currently has lots of eager buyers looking to acquire smaller players.

Number and Deadline

We calculate that $7.5 million creates the $250,000 passive income they want, funds the boys' educations fully, and gives them plenty of flexibility.

They want to be done with a post-sale earn-out within five years or less, so they hope to sell within three years.

Business Plan Highlights

Roy owns 40% of a software company he bootstrapped that does over $8 million in revenue. Roy figures the company is worth at least 2.5 times revenue, or about $20 million, because similarly sized competitors have sold for 4 or 5 times, but he'd rather be cautious.

In a modest $20 million sale, Roy's 40% would be worth about $8 million pre-tax. Let's assume $6 million after taxes.

The single biggest result his company must produce is 20/20: 20% EBITDA margins and a 20% revenue growth rate. Their EBITDA margins and growth rate are the #1, #2, and #3 business priorities.

Roy also needs to switch from a solo practitioner CPA to a larger accounting firm in preparation for the sale. He's been meaning to make the move for years, but now has the impetus to get it done.

One potential problem to solve is his 20% partner, Jim, who is going through a divorce. Jim wants to keep all his shares, but the divorce could force him to sell half (10% of the entire company). That could mean a multimillion-dollar buyout.

And then there are a bunch of corporate documents that were done by the attorney who did Roy's home closing 12 years ago. He has no idea if they are any good.

I recommend they kill two birds with one stone: get a few firms to review the documents and use that as a "dry run" to find the right legal team to help them sell the company.

Roy's Business LFF Plan
LFF = $7,500,000 within 5 years

	Key Issues	Next steps
➕	• Sell biz for $10 milliion (net $6m) in 3 years • Hit $8m revenue in 2 years • 20% EBITDA margin, 20% growth rate	• Get info on industry multiples from Frank (CFO) • Create 2-year revenue plan with team • Finance team needs to create margin expansion plan • Must renew those 10 big contracts up for renewal next year
➖	• Sales growth slows • Sally, new head of Sales, doesn't produce • Jim, 20% partner, gets divorced and settlement forces a buyout	• Keep foot on gas and do Sales Team 10-minute huddle 1/wk (not every 2 wks) • Have dinner with Sally to make sure success criteria and strategy are clear • Jim and I meet with CFO to talk about strategy.

	• How do I get bought out if I don't wake up? • Does the business look me-proof? • Do we need a bigger accounting firm?	• Email John (attorney) about it • Ask Emily (sold similar biz 1 year ago) how she did it • Ask Jeff (business coach) for advice on this
	• Current accounting firm may not have capabilities we need for sale • Original agreements were done by real estate attorney, not corporate law expert	• Interview 3 firms based on E.O. Forum recommendations • Get new legal team to do 360 review of these docs

Personal Plan Highlights

Roy already has personal liquid investments worth about $1.5 million, but they're invested in a haphazard, unfocused portfolio that isn't very tax-efficient.

If we refocus the portfolio and only earn 6% to 7% a year, he'll have $2 million within five years. That plus a reasonable sale ($6 million net) gets him his number and a little cushion.

That margin of safety means Roy doesn't need a perfect sale to create financial freedom. He can afford to negotiate more cash upfront or a shorter earnout.

But there's a problem to solve—Roy is significantly underinsured. He's making $250,000 a year, has a net worth of about $10 million, and has a private business worth a lot less without him, but he only has $1 million of life insurance. I'll work with his life insurance agent to fix that.

On top of that, Roy and his wife have never done wills or any kind of estate planning. We need to schedule a meeting right away with an attorney I trust to build an estate plan. That same attorney can also help minimize taxes when it's time to sell the business.

Roy and Lydia have a $300,000 rental property. They're not sure whether to sell it, 1031 exchange it into another property, or keep it.

We decide to sell it and reinvest the proceeds into a new property using a tax-free 1031 exchange. They don't need the money, but now they'll have more time to focus on it as a project (it's a fixer upper) post-sale.

Roy's Personal LFF Plan
LFF = $7,500,000 within 5 years

	Key Issues	Next steps
➕	• Personal investments grow to $2 million within 5 years • Minimize taxes on company sale • -Get financial house in order now so we can be financially worry-free once deal closes	• Create saving/investing strategy with Bill (financial advisor) • Set up planning meeting with CPA to run tax projections
➖	• I don't wake up tomorrow • Lydia doesn't know where all our financial stuff is • My parents need financial help	• Do life insurance review with Bill • Create doc that tells her who to call and where to find everything • Set up lunch with Mom + Dad to discuss

	• What to do with our rental property? • Enough for boys' undergrad? • How would we invest proceeds from selling the business to generate income? • Do we have too much or too little cash for an emergency?	• No idea where to start – Ask Bill
	• Property/casualty insurance broker stinks	• Ask Tom (savvy friend) for recommendations

Case Study #2—Karen: Built for Cash Flow

Karen is 54 and married with three kids. She and Nick wanted to talk to me because their financial life was "getting more complicated to manage," while their "time or inclination to manage it was shrinking."

Bottom line, even though they currently have two financial advisors, they feel they've outgrown those advisors' abilities. They "want someone to drive the bus."

Vision

Karen doesn't want to run her staffing business forever. The passion isn't there anymore, though cash flow is great. Ultimately, she plans to sell the business.

Nick wants to continue his family therapy practice, but on a much smaller scale.

Karen and Nick have no desire to stop working completely, but they want make work "financially irrelevant."

They've taken a lot of risk and are excited to live off money they don't have to actively earn. To get where they are, they had to "mortgage everything we could possibly borrow against" multiple times.

Karen is psyched to pursue new business adventures, while Nick can't wait to scale back his practice.

Number and Deadline

$20 million in seven years, when their youngest starts college. That will provide the roughly $750,000 pre-tax income they want.

They've saved quite a bit for college tuition, but feel they are "done funding college." The accounts will cover undergrad and possibly a Master's degree, but once they go to zero, Karen and Nick aren't paying any more.

Business Plan Highlights

Karen is 100% owner of a staffing business she founded. It's driven by her reputation in a few key industries, her deep relationships, and her unique abilities to help companies manage their growth.

She takes home about 20% of a $12 million top-line, or $2.5 million a year in personal income. The business is worth more in her hands than it is to a buyer, so Karen figures she could sell it for $3–5 million.

She has no desire to scale up the business and risk what is a high margin, low growth cash machine. She'd rather save money she can take out of the business and be less dependent on a monster sale.

Karen's business plan is to keep doing what they're doing and sustain flattish growth. The business is lumpy, so some years might do $15 million and some might do $10 million. Averaged out, $10–12 million ($2 million of personal income) is pretty sustainable, if not conservative.

The big focus over the next year is to close a few larger new clients in their pipeline. This could smooth out the lumpiness and potentially boost earnings significantly.

The biggest problem right now is a multimillion-dollar receivable an important Fortune 500 client owes them. It's been owed long enough for Karen to talk to her attorney.

She's also not sure her current CPA is cutting it, so I recommended she get a second opinion from a few local firms. She'll ask some fellow entrepreneurs for recommendations.

Karen's Business LFF Plan
LFF = $20,000,000 within 7 years

	Key Issues	Next steps
➕	• Generate minimum $2 million of income over next 7 years • Sell in 7 years for $3-5 million	• Close that big multi-year contract with XYZ Corporation • Ask Jack (CPA) what we can do this far in advance to minimize taxes
➖	• I don't wake up tomorrow • We lose Johnston Corp account • We never collect on that big receivable from our Fortune 500 client	• Create Emergency Plan with Carrie (controller) in QI • Schedule dinner with Paul Johnston soon • Schedule meeting w/Mark (attorney)
❓	• Who are the likely buyers? How can we develop a relationship now?	• Email John (attorney) about it
☺	• Not sure current CPA is cutting it	• Get second opinion on last 2 years' tax returns from 3 firms

Personal Plan Highlights

Karen and Nick save like crazy and are already somewhat diversified away from the business on an asset level, though not on an income level.

They save close to $1 million a year through Karen's 401(k), defined benefit plan, and personal investment accounts. Nick's therapy practice breaks even and he may start a small retirement plan soon.

Karen and Nick already have $4.2 million in liquid investments. If they add $1 million a year like they've been doing and grow those investments at 7% a year, that will be about $16 million in seven years.

There is another $1.5 million in illiquid, private investments like real estate and a few startups. Karen figures conservatively that they'll be worth $2 million in seven years. She plans on selling most of those over time to simplify the family balance sheet.

That will give them $18 million in seven years, so if selling the business nets $2 million after taxes, they'll hit their $20 million LFF number.

The biggest risk Karen's family faces is that she doesn't wake up. Karen's situation is the definition of key person risk, and there is no business value (except collecting receivables) if she dies.

Karen had some life and disability insurance, but not nearly enough to make her plan bulletproof. We will fix that in Phase 1 of our plan with their agent.

Karen and Nick have also been meaning to do a $500,000 renovation to their house. They have the cash, but they decide to hold off because, "If delaying the reno creates freedom faster, we're all in."

Karen and Nick also worry about their aging parents becoming a financial burden. They're not sure if Karen's parents are financially secure, and they are already supporting Nick's mother. We'll work through these issues in Phase 2.

Karen's Personal LFF Plan
LFF = $20,000,000 within 7 years

	Key Issues	Next steps
➕	• Personal investments grow to $15 million in 7 years • Get original investment back from Pam venture • The girls' college is funded by the time we sell the biz	• Discuss saving/investing strategy with Bill (advisor) • Set up planning meeting with CPA • Ask Bill if we should fund college savings plans or fund personal accounts
➖	• Something bad happens to me, I can't work anymore, and we put the business into liquidation (collect receivables, etc.) • Mom needs to move, and we get distracted • Our home remodel goes over budget and kills our savings plan	• Do life/disability analysis with Bill. Buy more insurance if needed. I want plan FULLY FUNDED no matter what happens to me. • Find a better permanent living situation for her that could handle her health declining • Talk to Nick about delaying remodel
❓	• Are we saving enough to hit $20m in 7 years? Does our current investment strategy make sense? • Are Nick's parents financially secure or will we need to assist them?	• Discuss with Bill • Take a walk with Nick's father next time we visit them and ask for transparency
☺	• Must update wills and estate plan but don't know who to call	• Ask Bill and business buddies for recommendations

What are you waiting for?

There are hundreds of other financial planning issues we could talk about. I could write three books with just case studies.

Roy and Karen clearly have different paths to LFF. Roy's path is built around selling his business, and Karen's is built around saving money.

No plan is inherently right or wrong, but there are clearly better or worse paths for you personally. I hope these case studies show how simple creating your plan can be if you start with the right questions.

Remember—people with a plan create lasting financial freedom; people without a plan don't.

Notice that I didn't say people with a "perfect" plan. A plan is better than no plan at all. Financial planning is about doing, not just knowing. Make planning a priority now. Get started, even if it just means scheduling 15 minutes on your calendar tomorrow. Even a basic sketch of a plan is a huge step forward.

You have the tools to help you build a bridge to lasting financial freedom, but it's up to you to start using them.

If you are planning to actually do the
three exercises (Vision-Number-Plan) in Part 1,
stop reading right now and go do them.

The rest of this book can wait.

Seriously. **STOP READING.**

Go do those exercises.

You can download the worksheets at
KnowYourNumberBonus.com.

PART 2

WORKING YOUR PLAN

You bought an acre of land, had blueprints drawn, hired a contractor to do the work, and have every building material you'll ever need ready to go.

Do you own a dream home yet?

No, of course not. Sure, the raw materials are there, but they haven't been assembled.

Financially, it is the same process. Even if you have the raw materials (cash equal to your LFF Number), it's **what you do with raw materials** that determines whether or not they become LFF.

Part One taught you how to gather the raw materials. Part Two will teach you how to turn those raw materials into lasting financial freedom, not just freedom for a while.

While Part One was more strategic and big picture. Part Two is more granular and technical. It offers you tactical, actionable ideas on what to do with your money.

Before You Invest a Dollar, Do This

> ❝ It's insane to risk what you have and need for something you don't really need. ❞
>
> *—Warren Buffett,*
> *Chairman of Berkshire Hathaway*

You created a plan and it worked. You're sitting on a big pile of cash. Congratulations! Now what?

How can you invest in a way that grows your money, secures your financial freedom, and also allows for future opportunities you might need capital to fund?

What I'm about to share is what you need to do to avoid big financial trouble after selling your company or achieving financial freedom.

Despite what you're thinking, the first question you should ask is not, "How should I invest my money?"

The first question you should ask is, "How should I *divide* my money?"

Divide your money first

After a huge liquidity event, you might think every business or investment you touch from now on will turn to gold. If you're not careful, a big check can make you forget that you're proven in one area and a beginner in other areas.

Remember when Michael Jordan played minor league baseball? He was the greatest basketball player in the world—if not of all time—but that meant little on the baseball field, where he was mediocre at best.

Dividing your money provides natural boundaries and risk management for the pile of cash you worked so hard to earn. It protects you as you learn to play a new game.

Your first step is to separate **what you need** from **what you don't need.** You can't invest every dollar the same way. That's how entrepreneurs end up on the get rich twice program—make it, blow it, make it again. I'd rather you get rich once.

First, you have a **freedom bucket.** It has one job—protecting your financial freedom.

You fill this bucket with cash you'll need to spend and investments that can produce an income stream for decades. Freedom-driven investments grow in % terms (7–10%), not X terms (2×, 5×, etc.). This is your family's cash cow.

This is "must win" money. Losing any of it would negatively impact your life—reduce your income, force you to work again, take future options away from you, etc.

That's why these investments should be liquid, broadly diversified, and simple (like mainstream stock funds). They're built to hit singles and doubles, not home runs. Typically, your wealth advisor manages the freedom bucket for you.

The other bucket, the **multiplier bucket**, could significantly multiply your financial freedom. This is what gets entrepreneurs really excited.

These are investments like startups, venture capital, real estate projects, or individual stocks that could grow 5×, 10×, or 100×. Multipliers tend to be ventures where you can influence outcomes or utilize your unique abilities.

Multipliers are highly illiquid (you can't get out easily), take a long time to produce a return, or could result in total losses.

It's not a mistake to invest in multipliers—it's a mistake to invest the *wrong dollars* in them. You invest money in multipliers that you can afford to lose without changing your life.

Multipliers can also multiply impact, not just financial freedom. Maybe there's a cause you want to support or a family you'd like to help out with some of the money you won't need.

Freedom	Multiplier
% growth (Ex: 7%)	X growth (Ex: 2×, 10×, 100×)
Liquid	Illiquid
Losses will change your life	Losses won't change your life
Diversified	Concentrated

What dividing your money looks like

Investing is about risk and reward. You need to know how much you can and can't lose.

So if your LFF number is $10 million and you have $10 million, all of it should go into freedom investments, unless you're eager to put your financial freedom at risk.

If you have $12 million, you could invest $10 million in the freedom bucket and still have up to $2 million to invest in multipliers. Even if you lose that $2 million or don't get it back for 10 years, your family's life doesn't change.

You could also give some of that $2 million to a charity you support.

The problem is when you invest all your money into multiplier investments, like Adam (from earlier in the book).

He hoped $15 million was going to turn into $100 million, but instead 80% vanished. That's how he became an alum of the "Get Rich Twice" school like many successful entrepreneurs.

The freedom/multiplier bucket concept should also help when you think about future ventures. That freedom bucket is sacred, but the multiplier bucket can leave room for spicier investments.

One overlooked benefit to the freedom bucket

It's not fun to think about what can go wrong, but you're being irresponsible if you don't assess risk as well as reward. Fortunately, having two buckets makes assessing risk a lot more comfortable.

Let's say your family needed $10 million to live comfortably, and you had $10 million in a freedom bucket and $5 million in the multiplier bucket. Let's also say that you get hit by a bus tomorrow. Forget the immense loss that would mean for your family for a moment and think purely in financial terms.

If you didn't wake up, nothing much would change in that freedom bucket. Your advisor could keep running it the same way so your family's financial needs were handled. Your advisor would meet with your spouse regularly, and those assets would be fine.

The multiplier bucket is another story. It requires your judgment to be successful, but your judgment is now gone. You left partnerships your spouse and advisor need to unwind or sell and assets they don't know what to do with. They might be in over their heads.

Here's the good news—thanks to the freedom/multiplier mix, your family still has the freedom bucket as a turnkey solution, even if they completely mismanage the multiplier bucket.

Your family will thank you for that. Having someone to keep your family's financial life in order without you is an often overlooked reason to hire a top-notch wealth advisor.

What about real estate?

Everybody loves real estate. But does it belong in the multiplier bucket or the freedom bucket? Well, that depends.

First off, real estate is just like any other investment. If you know what you're doing, you'll make money. If you don't, you can get creamed. So—do you have an edge?

My clients who are great real estate investors either have an **informational edge** (unique market insight, experience, relationships, zoning knowledge, etc.) or an **operational edge** (a proven process, own a management company, live nearby, can do repairs or renovations in-house or wholesale, etc.).

Second, what kind of real estate are you talking about? Dirt to be developed, condo conversions, a home to flip, an apartment building, or the second floor of an office building you own and use for your company?

Those each have very different risk/reward profiles.

Third, how bulletproof is the real estate in question? Owning one building with two short-term tenants (3- to 5-year leases) is a lot riskier than owning a bunch of buildings with 200 tenants or having one Fortune 500 tenant with a 15-year lease.

Bottom line, unless you made your money building a real estate portfolio, I'd put real estate in the multiplier bucket.

The Greatest Risk to Preserving Your Wealth

" Know your enemy and know yourself and you will always be victorious. **"**

—Sun Tzu,
author of The Art of War

LFF isn't a one-time event; it's an ongoing process. Your freedom bucket likely needs to produce income every single year for decades.

The difference between LFF and FF is how long it lasts. Enough money to not work for 20 years is FF. Enough money so you can do whatever you want even if you live to 120 is LFF.

Medicine keeps advancing, and people keep living longer. If you're married and don't smoke, the odds are high that at least one of you lives past 90. You may both live beyond 100 depending on your lifestyle, genetics, and access to great medical advice.

Let's say you're 50 years old. **For financial freedom to turn into *lasting* financial freedom, your freedom bucket may need to generate income for the next 40 or 50 years.**

(This should be eye-opening if you're selling a company in your 30s or 40s. In that case, you have 2–3× more life ahead of you than behind you.)

So how do you make sure a long life never becomes a financial risk?

The big risk hidden in plain sight

My wife and I recently took my 86-year-old grandmother out to lunch. (She tried raw oysters for the first time and loved them.)

Granny talked about how when she and Gramps were newlyweds, "We each made thirty dollars a week."

I was shocked. That was only $240/month, which wouldn't even cover my car payment, let alone my entire life.

I instantly recalled a similar story one of my mentors had shared about visiting the local Ford dealer in 1969 when his wife was pregnant with their first child.

That day he drove home with a fully loaded Ford Galaxy the size of a cruise ship. It cost $3,500.

Thirty years later, his firstborn went to the same dealership and bought a Ford Explorer. You know what she paid? $35,000.

Are you seeing a pattern here?

Rule #1 to investing your freedom bucket wisely is to know the enemy—and the enemy is constantly rising costs.

Almost everything you buy costs a little more every year. It's imperceptible in the short run, but it makes a huge difference in the long run.

Historically, living costs rise about 3% a year. At that rate, **everything doubles in price every 24 years.** So what costs $1 today would cost…

$2.40 in 30 years…

$3.26 in 40 years…

and $4.38 in 50 years.

So if you don't *at least* double or triple (or quadruple) your income over the rest of your life, then you have a plan for losing purchasing power, dramatically shrinking your lifestyle, and eventually running out of money.

That's why *lasting* financial freedom isn't easy to create.

If you put $10 million in the bank and still had that same $10 million years later while your living costs doubled, some people would say you successfully preserved your wealth.

Wrong. You preserved your *money* (currency units), but lost half your *purchasing power* (what those currency units can buy).

You cannot predict whether the market's next 20% move will be up or down, but you can be reasonably certain that the next 20%, 50%, or 100% move in your living costs will be up, not down. Even if your lifestyle doesn't increase one bit.

To me, the only sane definition of "wealth preservation" is **preserving your purchasing power**, not currency units, because everything costs more over time.

Likewise, "wealth creation" is *increasing* your purchasing power. That means you can afford to live a more expensive lifestyle in the future than you can today.

If preserving purchasing power (wealth preservation) is your goal—and it should be—then that will influence how you invest your freedom bucket.

What kind of investments are safe?

No matter where you open an investment account, you can probably choose from over 10,000 investment options.

Target-date, income, small-cap, large-cap, U.S., international, emerging markets, value, growth, active, index, long-short, long-only, currency-hedged…and that's just the beginning.

It's enough to feel completely overwhelmed. Luckily, everything on that list falls into two categories:

1. **Fixed income investments** like bonds, money market accounts, and certificates of deposit (CDs). For every dollar you loan, you earn a fixed interest payment for a promised period of time and then get your principal back.

2. **Rising income investments** like stock funds or income-producing real estate. You receive a stream of cash flow (dividends, rent, etc.) that rises over time, as well as any appreciation in the value of your investment.

But *fixed* income investments won't help you in a *rising* cost world.

That's why I worry when I hear big-time entrepreneurs say things like, "I take plenty of risk in my business, so I want my investments to be safe."

By "safe," they mean bonds, CDs, etc. But here's why that's actually a very dangerous idea.

Since 1926, government bonds have returned about 5.5% a year.[2] Large-cap stocks have done 10% annually and small-cap stocks have grown 12% a year.[3]

So right off the bat, you see stock returns (10–12%) roughly *doubled* bond returns (5.5%) before inflation.

When you factor in 3% inflation (remember, we want to maintain purchasing power), bonds returned about 2.5% while stocks returned 7–9%.

In other words, adjusted for inflation, stocks roughly *tripled* what bonds returned. Clearly, owning companies is a lot more profitable over time than loaning to them. But you already knew that.

If rising costs are *the* long-term threat to your freedom, then **investments that maintain or grow your purchasing power are safest** in the long run.

Bonds are hazardous to your long-term financial health the same way smoking is to your physical health.

Stocks can generate tremendous income over time. Since 1960, just the cash dividend growth on the S&P 500 has roughly doubled the inflation rate (5.5% or so).[4] So even while share prices are wiggling around, your "rent checks" keep pace with rising costs and then some.

The bottom line?

Believing the conventional wisdom that "bonds are safe, stocks are risky" won't build an income stream that can support you for decades.

While that doesn't necessarily mean you should *never* own bonds, it does mean that anyone who tells you bonds are safe doesn't understand risk.

You want an engine to protect purchasing power? Owning high-quality companies from around the world will give you all the horsepower you need.

An example of the rising income engine at work

My mom and dad got married on October 6, 1974.

Let's imagine they got home from their honeymoon, wrote their thank you notes, and invested wedding gifts in an S&P 500 fund on November 1, 1974. The S&P closed at 71 that day.[5]

Since Mom and Dad were young and just starting out, we'll assume they had to spend dividends (no reinvesting) but never sold the shares.

For their first full year of dividends in 1975, they received **$3.73** for every share they bought.

In 1980, Mom gave birth to an almost 11-pound baby boy who practically killed her (sorry, Mom). But their dividends were now **$6.44** a share, up over 70% in about five years.

By the time I graduated high school in 1998, the dividend hit **$16.20**. When I married my beautiful wife, Emma, in 2007, it was **$27.73**. And by 2016, each share was throwing off just over **$45** a year in dividends.

So what happened during those 42 years of marriage?

My parents' living costs grew about 3.5×, so they needed a 3.5× increase to preserve purchasing power.[6]

But while costs grew 3.5✕, their dividend stream grew **12✕** (from $3.73 to $45) and the shares grew **31✕**. (The S&P went from 71 to 2,238.)

That's a huge increase in purchasing power, or wealth creation.

I'm not saying to put all your money in the S&P 500, but doesn't an income engine like that sound nice for your freedom bucket?

How to Earn
Real-Life Returns

> **"** The investor's chief problem—and his worst enemy—is likely to be himself. In the end, how your investments behave is much less important than how you behave. **"**
>
> —*Benjamin Graham,*
> *author of* Security Analysis *and* The Intelligent Investor,
> *widely known as the "father of value investing"*

We live in an investment culture obsessed with market timing, investment selection, and relative investment performance. It wants us to believe that creating LFF is based on our ability (or our advisor's ability) to:

1. **Predict** what happens next in the market or economy (Headline: "When Joe Guru thinks the current bear market will begin!")

2. **Pick** the best-performing stocks, funds, or managers (Headline: "Why XYZ Corp is going higher!")

3. **Time** markets, so you get in and out at the right moment (Headline: "Why now is a great time to sell!")

You don't need to bother reading that nonsense because LFF doesn't require predictive powers. Creating lasting financial freedom is based on what *you* do, not what your investments do.

Why?

Posted returns vs. real-life returns

Most investors assume the returns the *investment* earned are the same as the returns the fund's *investors* earned.

For example, if the Skywalker Growth Fund returned 12% a year, you assume the fund's investors earned 12% a year.

But that's not what happens in real life. Not even close.

Every year, an independent research firm named Dalbar studies how living, breathing investors like you and me buy and sell mutual funds.

Dalbar's study found that if you bought the world's most mundane equity investment (the S&P 500) in January 1985, automatically reinvested dividends, and forgot about it for three decades (December 2014), you earned **11.06%** annually.

So investors as a whole earned 11% a year, right?

Wrong. That's how the *investment* did, not how *investors* did.

How did the equity mutual fund investors do? They earned **3.79%** per year during those same three decades.

Over 30 years, the average investor underperformed the S&P 500 by *over 7% a year.* They lost more than half the annual return.

But compounded it gets even worse.

The average investor turned $1 million into **$3,052,568** instead of over **$23,266,447** (S&P 500)[7].

$20 million gone. Investors lost 87% of the return. Ouch.

Oh, and by the way, you made *half* of your $23+ million in the last seven years of that 30-year period. You invest long-term because you make most of your money later on.

The truth about investing for real-life returns

Did investors do poorly because they picked the wrong funds?

Dalbar comes to the same conclusion every year—investors not only underperform the market, they underperform their own investments.

They buy and sell at the wrong time for the wrong reasons. Dalbar said:

> "Investment results are more dependent on investor behavior than fund performance."

It's so important I need to say it again—real-life investment results are more dependent on *investor behavior* than fund performance.

So even if you pick great long-term investments, bad behavior steals most of your return.

It's easy to forget that "down a lot in a hurry" can also mean "up a lot in a hurry," as well as "up a lot over time."

Behavioral science has proven that the pain of losing money is far greater than the pleasure of making it. That's a big reason why our brains don't process market declines very well. They jump into survival mode and try desperately to get us to sell.

Volatility is completely normal

The financial media treats volatility like a plague to be avoided. In reality, it's a perfectly normal part of life like holiday weight gain, rush-hour traffic, or weird relatives.

Let's look at the S&P 500 since 1980. Roughly one in four calendar years posted negative returns, according to J.P. Morgan Asset Management's quarterly *Guide to the Markets*.

On top of that, the *average* intra-year decline (peak to trough) was about 14%.

(A $10 million account temporarily declining to $8.6 million was normal, not noteworthy. Pause for a moment and think about how your stomach might feel at the sound of that news.)

One in six years had declines of over 20%. Those are scary—the four declines that were actually over 30% are especially scary.

So what's the pattern? There was no pattern except that every single decline proved *temporary*.

In the long run, **owning a global mix of high-quality companies** means owning living, breathing, growing, operating businesses that choose to be publicly traded instead of privately held.

Going public doesn't make them fundamentally different than private businesses. It just means they are larger than most and their shares trade daily.

Markets get way ahead of themselves in booms, and they fall way behind at panicked bottoms. But over time, businesses as a whole produce an ever-increasing stream of earnings and dividends, which raises their company values, and thereby raises their stock prices.

Why? Populations grow around the world, innovation continues, productivity rises, and earnings are reinvested to produce more future earnings.

The long-term trend is knowable (it's up), but the short-term movements around that trend are random and unknowable. So what?

A better formula for real-life returns

If you're going to sustain LFF, you don't have an *investment* problem—you have an *investor* problem.

You need to change your mental model of what investing is. Here's my formula:

$$\text{(Investment return)} - \text{(Behavior)} = \text{(Investor return)}$$
$$A B C$$

Most of us think investing is about asking, "How do I increase investment returns (A)?"

But it's really about making sure behavior (B) doesn't rob your real-life return (C).

For example, let's plug the Dalbar study into the formula:

$$11.06\% - 7.27\% = 3.79\%$$
investment return   *bad behavior*   *investor return*
$$A B C$$

Okay, so investor behavior is important. Still, you're itching to jack up investment performance (A), aren't you? You beat the odds in your business, so you'd like to beat the odds in your investments.

What if you picked the best-performing mutual fund over a 10-year period? Wouldn't that override this behavioral nonsense?

Well, let's see. Between 2000 and 2009, the #1 performing equity mutual fund earned over 18% a year[8]. But investors in the fund *lost* 11% a year on average…even though they bought the #1 fund.

Why? Because it was a volatile fund that took investors on a wild ride. Only those with nerves of steel proved capable of withstanding the dips and reaping the full return. Huge swings caused most investors to make more behavioral mistakes than usual.

What would Warren do?

Clearly, choosing "winning" investments may not get you great results.

That's why *investor behavior,* not investment performance, is the key to real-life returns that can create your LFF engine.

Even Warren Buffett, who has loads of IQ, agrees:

> *"The most important quality for an investor*
> *is temperament, not intellect."*

You don't necessarily need to *pick* investments like Warren Buffett. You just need to *behave* like Warren Buffett over a really long time.

That's not easy. So how do you make sure you act like Warren year in and year out?

How to Stay Disciplined for Decades

> **"** Everyone has a plan until they get punched in the mouth. **"**
>
> *—Mike Tyson,*
> *former undisputed heavyweight champion*

If you own a private business or an apartment building, you don't get an update on its value every day. But publicly traded investments give you a quoted price every trading day. And those quotes may not reflect fair value for long stretches.

Those constantly moving red and green numbers are the root cause of bad investor behavior.

Think about it. If you watched a market decline day after day, which of the following are you more likely to think?

- **Option 1:** *This decline from $3 million to $2 million is temporary. No big deal. I should add whatever extra cash I can find before this sale ends.*

- **Option 2:** *I just lost a million dollars! I'd better sell and keep my $2 million safe until the smoke clears.*

Option one is rational, but option two is *human nature*. That's why most investors panic, sell, and mishandle the opportunity volatility has gifted them.

Your greatest enemies as an investor

Getting in shape is hard. Staying in shape is harder. Eventually, emotions and impulses win over rationality and discipline.

Unfortunately, behavioral mistakes are way costlier in investing than in other areas of life. If you eat a few donuts on Sunday but get back on the wagon Monday, you haven't permanently derailed your fitness.

But in investing, *even one mistake* made at a critical moment (when the temptation is greatest) can torpedo a lifetime of hard work.

And due to the power of compound interest, just a single year of inaction can cost you huge dollars down the road.

That's what makes emotions and impulses your greatest enemies as an investor—even when you detect their presence.

Remember that smart guy Adam who sold at the bottom? Do you think he knew that was a bad idea? Probably, but he sold anyway.

We can all be rational in theory, but it's hard to keep investing rationally over a lifetime. So how do you avoid the behavioral mistakes that so often toss LFF out the window?

You need a coach

You don't need a Chief Market Timer, Chief Fund Handicapper, or Chief Economic Prognosticator.

What you need is a Chief Behavioral Coach. (Though their business card might say wealth advisor, financial advisor, or wealth manager.)

Sure, your coach will help you create a plan for creating financial freedom (Vision-Number-Purpose-Plan), and design a portfolio of high-quality investments to protect that freedom.

Your coach will also make sure the advisors within your personal financial ecosystem (investments, insurance, tax, legal, etc.) are talking to one another. You don't really have a team until the players are communicating.

But that's only 20% of what he does for you. The other 80% is coaching you to stay disciplined not just for years, but for decades.

Your coach gets you to hold on and buy more through widespread panics like the 2008–2009 financial crisis, cools you off during the euphoria of the dot-com boom, and puts things in perspective when personal struggles may cloud your vision.

When your windshield gets muddy in a bear market, your advisor is there to wipe it off and keep you calm, cool, and rational. You can *feel* all the fear or euphoria you want, but your coach won't let you act on it.

Most people think you hire an advisor to maximize your investment return. That's why most people think the best question to ask a prospective advisor is, "What's your investment track record?"

But the answer is irrelevant. A well-constructed, goal-driven portfolio won't fall short for you because of relative investment performance—it will fall short because of bad behavior.

(Not to mention, there is no way to scientifically pick which funds will outperform in the future based on past performance.)

World-class performers, whether they're athletes or musicians or entrepreneurs, have coaches to offer specialized expertise, perspective, strategy, feedback, accountability, and a kick in the butt when they need it.

Michael Phelps won 23 Olympic gold medals because he's an amazing swimmer, but also because of a 20-plus-year relationship with his coach, Bob Bowman.

Steve Jobs, Larry Page, and Jeff Bezos relied on counsel from "coach" Bill Campbell before he passed away a few years ago.

Verne Harnish, founder of the Entrepreneurs' Organization (EO) and author of *Scaling Up: How a Few Companies Make it...and Why the Rest Don't*, once said:

> *"No one has achieved peak performance without a coach."*

In fact, Dr. Atul Gawande, author of *The Checklist Manifesto* (among other bestsellers), wrote an article for *The New Yorker* saying:

> *"Coaching done well may be the most effective intervention designed for human performance."*[9]

A coach can see clearly from the sidelines what you aren't able to see on your own when you're playing the game.

I have coaches for two critical areas in my life—fitness and business. And neither one of them comes cheap.

Is it possible I could get great results without them? Sure, but it's not probable. And I'm serious about getting results in those areas. I can't risk messing them up.

The ROI of a coach

Value is when you get a lot more than what you paid.

Let's assume you had a financial advisor for the last 30 years whose only move was keeping you in the S&P 500. How much return did you pick up over most investors? The Dalbar study says about 7% a year.

What would an advisor have charged in return for that pick-up? Probably around 1% a year, depending on your account size, to keep you from making mistakes that eroded your returns.

That sounds like a no-brainer, even before considering everything else your advisor would have done during that period:

- Figuring out your LFF number and creating a plan for achieving it.
- Helping you to maximize the biggest financial event of your life—selling your business.

- Working with your accountant or tax attorney to reduce your tax bill.

- Talking you out of that private investment that went bust for your friends.

- Convincing you to finally take action on that estate plan you've "snoozed" for years.

- Uncovering how vulnerable you were financially and working with your insurance agent to fix it.

- Encouraging you to have the talk with your siblings about your aging parents' health and financial needs so you can have peace of mind about their future.

- Giving your youngest daughter advice about her employee benefits and retirement plan so she can start her financial journey on the right track.

Your advisor bridges the "should" gap—that chasm between *what you know you should do* and *what you actually do* in real life—and highlights dangers or opportunities you missed.

When that happens, you're free to do what you do best and enjoy doing most.

No advice is dangerous. Bad advice is expensive. But great advice is a bargain.

How to Find Your Coach

" Get the right people on the bus and in the right seat. **"**

—Jim Collins,
author of Good to Great

Realizing you need a coach is one thing, but actually finding a good one is another. With so many options, it can feel overwhelming. How do you find the right fit from the hundreds of thousands of choices available to you around the country?

Getting the right people on the bus was one of the key principles in Jim Collins' *Good to Great.* You may be great at hiring for your business, but how do you hire a financial advisor?

You ask the right questions.

Get some recommendations of candidates from friends in a similar financial position (not friends with way more or way less money), and ask candidates these questions:

1. Are you legally required to act in my best interests?

Surely you'd only consider an advisor required to act in your best interest. The fancy term is "fiduciary."

Fiduciaries are paid fees directly from you (usually a percentage of assets). All the great advisors I know operate like that, while all the bad advisors I've seen "earn" commissions from steering people into products.

By the way, I trust my accountant and my attorney with my life. But I've never heard them brag about being fiduciaries.

Some advisors now use "fiduciary" as a marketing tool. Honesty isn't something you brag about—if you meet someone who does this, run in the opposite direction.

2. Can you help me make decisions across my entire financial picture, or just on investments or insurance?

You need comprehensive, total picture planning, so you need a *Certified Financial Planner*™ *or CFP*®. That program covers everything from investments to taxes to estate planning to insurance.

It's like an MBA in personal finance, and only 25% of financial advisors have the designation.[10] So you've already eliminated 75% of candidates. I think it's a total no-brainer decision.

3. Do you specialize in helping entrepreneurs like me?

I don't want a dentist doing my heart surgery, a brain surgeon doing my knee replacement, or a pediatrician fixing my teeth. I want someone who does that one thing all day long.

Many financial advisors work with almost anyone. Better advisors work only with larger "high net worth" accounts, but that's not a specialty.

High net worth entertainers or athletes face different issues than families who inherited wealth. And public company CEOs have different challenges than founders of private companies.

Find an advisor who specializes in helping entrepreneurs just like you. A specialist is better equipped to understand your mindset, your goals, your vulnerabilities, and solve the technical problems you face.

4. Are you focused on beating the market or do you take a behavior-driven approach?

There's no scientific way to predict which advisor can maximize investment performance. And, as we've seen, it's not wise to just hire the one who promises the highest returns.

But you can probably pick the advisor you feel will help manage you best at critical moments. Ask yourself, "Which one do I like and trust enough to keep me on the program year in and year out?"

Who is going to get you to focus on and master the fundamentals with incredible discipline?

5. Could I work with you as a long-term business partner?

The right advisor is a trustworthy partner, not merely a service provider. He has your back through thick and thin. He is as committed to your success as you are. He complements your own strengths and weaknesses.

Most of all, a partner is someone who cares about you, not just your money.

A partner isn't afraid to disagree with you. Avoid the "order taker" who never pushes back. That's an enabler, not a partner.

Don't settle for a B player. Find the A player who's a great fit.

Warning: 4 big mistakes people make when hiring an advisor

Now that you know what to do, here's a list of what *not* to do.

1. Going the robo route

"Robo-advisors" are financial advisors the same way TurboTax is a trusted accountant and tax strategist—they're not.

Robos are just electronic portfolio management. If you're lucky, you get access to a call center of strangers ("financial experts"). Would you hire an attorney from a call center to help you sell your company?

Portfolio management matters, but it's a small piece of what you need an advisor to do. An advisor helps you clarify goals, creates a holistic financial plan (not just investing), and provides behavioral investment guidance so emotions don't rob your returns.

Most troubling to me, though, is what might happen at major market downturns with a robo. Will the robot intervene or just let you panic and sell? (Does your FitBit stop you from eating donuts?)

At best, robo-advisors are a dressed-up DIY solution. And in financial planning, DIY can easily turn into BIY—blow it yourself.

2. Collecting advisors like baseball cards

You'll never hear a smart CEO say:

> *"I have three CFOs. I don't really trust
> any of them, so I'm diversifying."*

That sounds nuts. Yet many wealthy entrepreneurs hire (or keep) multiple financial advisors because they want to "diversify." Guess what? Your portfolio is not diversified because you have multiple advisors.

I know, I know—it *feels* diversified getting different statements from different institutions. But feeling diversified isn't the same as *being* diversified.

I've sat down with lots of wealthy families using multiple advisors at big firms over the years, and here's what I've found:

1. There were huge holes and redundancies.

2. There was no overarching financial plan.

3. They were paying way more in fees than necessary.

4. They were more stressed and confused about their money than most folks I meet.

Nowadays, you can get all the portfolio diversification you'll ever need with one advisor. Just choose wisely.

3. Running a performance derby

The worst version of the multiple advisor problem is the performance derby—you give three advisors some money, see how they do, and the person with the best returns at the end gets all of your business.

The truth is you won't actually learn anything from a performance derby. In fact, it only opens you up to more risk. Here's why:

- The "winner" may have taken way more risk to get more return, increasing your odds of a blowup.

- The "winner" may have won because his investment style (value, growth, small, large, U.S., global) was in favor over that period.

- The "winner" of this period doesn't predict who will win over the next period of time.

Relative investment performance pales in comparison to investor behavior.

Remember that #1 fund that earned 18% a year while its investors lost 11% a year?

If you're down 25% while the S&P 500 is down 35%, you're "beating the S&P" by 10%. But that "outperformance" won't matter a lick if you press the panic button and cash out.

4. Staying with someone you've outgrown

Hiring the wrong person happens. But sticking with a person after you *know* they're wrong is a huge mistake. (And people usually do it just to avoid one uncomfortable conversation.)

Maybe you've outgrown your advisor. That's a part of life and it means big things have happened for you.

Or maybe you've hesitated on consolidating to one advisor you trust because the other one is a "really nice guy."

Remember, it's *your* money. You worked hard for it. You deserve to have it handled right. If you wouldn't re-hire the person you have, invest the time and effort to find the right one.

What a Freedom Portfolio Looks Like

After behavior and temperament, portfolio structure is the biggest reason people invest poorly.

What investment decisions maximize your chances of creating a freedom-protecting portfolio without taking on unnecessary risk?

Entire books have been written on the subject, but there are four no-brainer decisions that will easily put you miles ahead.

----

1. You're focused on the right mix

Your stock/bond mix will be *the most important investment decision* governing your lifetime returns. (Read that again.)

Common sense tells you owning more 10–12% return assets (stocks) than 5–6% return assets (bonds) will increase your portfolio's lifetime return. Well, research confirms that hunch. Some studies say asset allocation (the fancy term for your stocks/bonds/cash mix) accounts for over 90% of your portfolio's return.[11]

One study by Ibbotson even said asset allocation accounted for *over 100%* of portfolio return. How? Because timing and selection had a net *negative* impact on returns.

(That study should be another not-so-subtle message that market timing is a dumb idea.)

2. You're diversified properly

Your portfolio's job is to generate a rising income that sustains your lifestyle over the long haul. Since you don't need the highest returns in the universe to do that, diversifying is a no-brainer.

My mentor, Nick Murray, has been in the financial industry for over 50 years and written 12 books on the subject. He defines diversification better than anyone:

> *"Diversification is the conscious choice never to make a killing in exchange for the blessing of never getting killed."*

Individual businesses can (and do) go to zero. That's why it's wise to own a bunch of businesses that, as a whole, won't lose money over time. So put your serious money into **funds**, not individual stocks. (Get your kicks in your multiplier bucket if you must.)

Next, you want to own individually attractive assets with similar long-term growth expectations that may run on different cycles. Why?

Between 2000 and 2009, the S&P 500 *lost* about 1% a year (dividends reinvested). The media called it the "lost decade," but that wasn't entirely true for other categories.[12]

During that same decade, U.S. small-cap value indexes more than doubled. Emerging markets stocks and U.S. REITs (real estate investment trusts) were up more than 2.5×.

That's why you diversify.

A freedom-driven portfolio should have small companies (like a young Starbucks), non-U.S. companies (harness globalization), and a balance of value (lower-priced tortoises) and growth (higher-priced hares).

You want high-quality ingredients that are great on their own, but even better when properly assembled. They'll zig and zag at different times, but that's the point.

3. You buy for keeps

When Warren Buffett visits MBA students each year, he advises them to act as if they had a lifetime decision card with 20 punches on it.

After investment number 20, you can't make another investment. He says:

> *"Under those rules, you'd really think carefully about what you did, and you'd be forced to load up on what you'd really thought about. So you'd do so much better."*

Most people think Berkshire Hathaway shareholders are rich solely because of Buffett's investment ability. But they miss how Buffett trained shareholders to think of those shares as a forever holding.

Again, it all comes back to *behavior*.

If Berkshire Hathaway had been half as successful, shareholders would still be quite rich because of the behavior Buffett ingrained. (Not *as* rich, but still plenty rich.)

Don't ask, "Where should I invest now?" That's a renter mentality.

Instead ask, "What could I be happy owning forever?" You'll make fewer, better decisions.

4. You use two simple, powerful tools

The Dalbar study showed that investors consistently underperform their own investments. It would be great to get the actual returns of your investments, but is *outperforming* them even possible?

Dollar-cost averaging is the surest way to turn volatility into a profit center because it automates value investing.

By adding the same amount each month, you effortlessly buy teacups full of hotter, fully priced investments and barrels full of unsexy, cheaply priced investments.

But what if you're no longer accumulating? That's when you hire dollar-cost averaging's cousin—**rebalancing**.

Over time, a portfolio mix gets out of whack. Rebalancing trims the hot ones that just had a great run, and redeploys cash into the colder ones that may be ready for a run. You systematically buy low and sell high.

Rebalancing and dollar-cost averaging mean you never need a market outlook or economic forecast. They do all the work for you.

What's the opposite of these tools? Market timing and performance chasing.

Performance chasing is selling what's cold to buy what's been on fire lately (manager, sector, commodity, stock, etc.).

Market timing is trading (getting in or out) based on a short-term viewpoint. Warren Buffett's words on the topic: *"I've never met a man who could time the market."* Enough said.

Don't speculate—invest. Bottom line.

Should you invest in index funds or active funds?

If serious money goes into funds, the question becomes, "Which funds?"

Active funds that attempt to beat the market by picking stocks or timing market cycles? Or **index funds** that provide market-mirroring returns without the possibility of outperformance?

I feel index funds are a great choice for the lion's share of your equity portfolio for five reasons:

1. They keep your *focus* where it should be—your stock/bond mix and your behavior—instead of trying to beat the market.

2. They *outperform* the vast majority of active funds over time. Over the last 15 years, **92%** of large-cap managers and **93%** of small-cap managers *trailed* their benchmark.[13]

3. They are more *tax-efficient* than active funds due to low turnover.

4. They eliminate *manager risk*. Your favorite active fund manager can easily leave, get fired, or get so big that great ideas can't move the needle.

5. They eliminate *style drift*. You don't have to worry, for example, about small-cap value stocks wandering into your large-cap growth fund.

Index funds are the lowest risk, most effective way to invest in global equities over the rest of your lifetime. They also pass the Buffett "forever holding" test.

Is it wrong to invest money in active funds? Of course not. I may prefer indexing the majority of your portfolio, but I'm not a zealot. In the long run, investor behavior overrides investment selection.

Sound too simple?

What most advisors won't tell you is that investing actually *is* simple. It's doing it consistently over an entire lifetime that's so hard. Behavior, behavior, behavior.

How to Make Volatility Meaningless

> ❝ The man who is prepared has his battle half fought. ❞
>
> —*Miguel de Cervantes,*
> *author of* Don Quixote

Behavior. Check. Portfolio structure. Check.

The only obstacle left on your way to LFF? Poor planning that leaves you short on cash and forces you to sell investments at a fire sale during a temporary decline.

Even with a strong financial foundation, there's still one perfectly legitimate fear you may have:

What if I invest a big payday right before a major decline?

You can't predict when or why downturns will happen, but you *can* make them financially (and psychologically) meaningless through smart planning.

Imagine you sell your company (or a big asset) in summer 2008, and you're sitting on a big pile of cash. The financial crisis hits and your portfolio takes a beating. Uh oh.

The technical term for this scenario is "sequence of returns" risk. It's the risk that a few early negative return years make you run out of money.

The good news is you can successfully navigate it with a little extra planning. By mixing and matching the following five strategies, you'll turn any meltdown into a non-event—even if it happens when you need your investments the most.

1. MUST: The 5/4/3 spending plan

First, any you'll need *within five years* for "one and done" expenses (like college tuition, weddings, special trips or experiences, or kitchen remodels) should NOT be invested. Keep that stash in short-term cash equivalents.

Second, only draw *4% a year* (max) as income so you don't spend yourself into full liquidation.

Third, when you start living off your assets, keep *three years* of living expenses in cash.

Why three years? Because historically that would have given you a big enough war chest to not only weather any temporarily declines but also sleep well at night. Even during tough times like the 2008 crisis.

Cash is like oxygen. When there is enough in the room, you don't notice it. When there isn't enough, it's the *only* thing you notice.

2. MUST: A bear market battle plan

You and your advisor can decide in advance on a tripwire (percentage decline) that triggers a bear market battle plan.

For example, when a panic hits and your account is temporarily down 25%, you'll do some combination of the following:

1. Shut down withdrawals entirely and live off your three-year cash reserves.

2. Live on dividends only and supplement with cash reserves.

3. Hold living costs steady or limit discretionary spending (travel, fun, etc.) until the dust settles.

Are you starting to see why people with a plan make it and people without plans don't?

You can't predict bear markets, but you can plan for them.

3. OPTIONAL: Dollar-cost average into your portfolio

Earn-out payments can be an automatic dollar-cost averaging strategy. You get half up front, and then you invest the other half slowly over the next few years.

But when you get all the money up front, emotions can cloud your decision-making.

Statistically, you're better off investing a lump sum right away since returns are positive about 75% of calendar years. Psychologically, though, it's perfectly sensible to have a dollar-cost average plan for a big check.

For example, you get a check for $5 million. Here are a few possible plans:

- Invest $3 million and then $100,000/month for 20 months.

- Invest $1 million up front and then $1 million/quarter for a year.

- Invest $200,000/month for two years.

Schedule your investments (weekly, monthly, quarterly) so they are automatic. Don't try to get cute with timing payments—skip this month, invest more next month, etc. That's market timing, not planning.

That said, you could always *accelerate* the plan if you get the opportunity to buy high-quality merchandise at a discount during a big decline.

4. OPTIONAL: Gradually bring your portfolio to target

This is a variation on the dollar-cost averaging plan. Let's say your LFF portfolio will be 90% equities, 10% bonds.

You could start with 30% bonds, cut bonds to 20% in year two, and trim once more to 10% in year three. (In other words, increase equities from 70% to 90%.)

If you hit a downturn right away and need extra cash, you could sell pieces of the bonds and give the equities time to recover. Sure, you might miss out on some returns if your portfolio goes straight up for a few years, but at least you'll have protected LFF.

5. OPTIONAL: Gradually bring spending to target

Yes, this is the least fun strategy, but it's an effective strategy nonetheless.

If your spending target is low (think 2-3% of your assets) it won't be necessary. But if your spending target is at or close to the 4% annual limit, you could gradually increase it from 3% to 3.5% to 4% over a few years in order to further reduce risk in the early years after you create LFF.

If you're fortunate enough to create the wealth we've talked about, a high percentage of your spending is likely wants, not needs. Capping your spending in the short-term to eliminate long-term risk can be a smart trade-off.

How to Invest Your Multiplier Bucket Like a Boss

> ❝ Terribly smart people make totally bonkers mistakes. ❞
>
> *—Charlie Munger,*
> *billionaire and long-time business*
> *partner of Warren Buffett*

By now, you have a clear understanding of how to invest the freedom bucket—the money you live on and can't afford to lose.

But what about the multiplier bucket, that money you can use to pursue other investment opportunities?

How do you invest in real estate, other businesses, or opportunities you may come across without losing your shirt?

I've seen my clients invest in multipliers successfully, and I've seen them invest in multipliers disastrously. Here are the big mistakes I've seen and how to fix them.

MISTAKE: Dabbling by saying "yes" to everything

Risk comes from not knowing what you're doing. Selling a business for a lot of money feels great, but it's not exactly a lesson in humility. It's seductive to think that the skills that made you that money will turn you into a real estate mogul or a world-class angel investor.

Pros are clear about what they do know and even clearer about what they don't know. Amateurs dabble in a little bit of everything and call it diversifying.

Because you bump into so much opportunity as an entrepreneur, it's easy say to yes to everything. Don't.

FIX: Assume "no" unless it's amazing

Chris Sacca is a billionaire because he's one of the best venture investors of all time. (And no, you're not Chris Sacca or Warren Buffett).

His advice couldn't be clearer—when you're presented with an investment opportunity, **your default answer should be "no," not "yes."** It's just like Warren Buffett's "wait for the fat pitch" advice.

Fortunes are kept through discipline and focus. Fortunes are blown by wandering off and investing in things you don't really understand. Make fewer, bigger decisions with multiplier money. You don't need to find one every month or even every year.

That said, if you're investing in an area where you're a beginner but don't want to be forever (say real estate), you should start small, make mistakes with kid money, learn, and scale up slowly over time.

MISTAKE: Going with your gut

You built a business by following your instincts. Sure, they're not always right, but overall the results have been good.

Investing, however, is very different from running a business. You're putting money at risk with a lot less information than you had when you ran your business. A lot of "instinct" in business is just knowing so much about every little detail of your company. That's why your judgment was great overall.

Most of the time, "going with your gut" on an investment is just an excuse to do very little due diligence and jump in too quickly.

FIX: Create an investment checklist

Great investors, from Warren Buffett to Silicon Valley venture capitalists, have a mental checklist they use before they make an investment. Buffett looks for a business he can understand, great management already in place, a wide economic moat, and an attractive price.

His big mistakes over the years (he isn't perfect) occurred when he didn't follow that checklist, or only got three out of four items.

Build your own checklist that you have to review before pulling the trigger. That way, you won't accidentally end up in investments you regret later. Better to have too demanding a checklist than too lax a checklist.

Your sample checklist could look like this:

1. An industry where I have unique insight like _____

2. I can influence the outcome

3. Even if it doesn't go well, I can still earn _____%+ a year

4. I can get _____% of my initial investment back within _____years

MISTAKE: Obsess over minimizing taxes

Being tax-sensitive and tax-efficient is smart. Hating taxes so much that you never take chips off the table when you're up big is not smart.

How can I tell when someone is letting taxes cloud judgment? When they quote the *dollar amount* of taxes they'd have to pay instead of the *percentage amount*.

"But I'd have to pay $1 million in taxes!"

FIX: Obsess over managing risk

If you're fortunate and smart enough to have some home runs, congrats. To cash in, you have to pay some taxes…hopefully a lot.

For example, if you invest in something that rockets to a 5×, take 2× off the table and let the other 3× ride. Failing to do this is how some real estate investors got crushed in 2008. They bought real estate with very little money down, it shot up fast, they leveraged properties to buy more and more, and then it all crashed and burned.

That same story happens in all sorts of asset classes, whether it's a stock sector, real estate in one hot area, or a type of business that's the unicorn of the moment.

Pros understand the power of concentration, but they are ruthless about knowing when to take some money off the table. Think in percentages ("I'll pay 20% to make the other 80% safe"), not dollar amounts.

You're not "investing" when one bullet could kill your portfolio. Even if the revolver has 100 empty chambers, one bullet is still deadly.

MISTAKE: Getting fixated on the upside

We entrepreneurs are an excitable bunch. And our relentless optimism is what gets us through the tough times.

But this can make it easy for us to make mistakes with investments that get us pumped.

It's okay to get excited, but do this fix first.

FIX: Do a pre-mortem

A postmortem examines a body for cause of death. A pre-mortem allows you to examine your investments for cause of death before you ever invest.

Imagine yourself three years from now. You just got a call that this investment blew up and you lost all your money. What happened? What went wrong? Who was the problem? What did we miss?

Or ask yourself, "How can I blow up this investment? If I were a competitor or a bad guy, how would I take this out at the knees?"

This is a simple, easy thinking tool to help you focus on the downside.

3 Simple Things You Can Do Next

  ❝ Don't just think. Don't just talk. Don't just dream. None of that matters. The only thing that matters is what you do. **❞**

—*Jocko Willink, former Navy SEAL*

From the bottom of my heart, I hope you've enjoyed this book. I put a lot of work into it so that you could learn some valuable lessons quickly.

Understanding the steps to achieving LFF already puts you ahead of the vast majority of people who can only hope to take control of their financial future. But that head start is ultimately meaningless without action. Fortunately, you can get started without making any big decisions or time commitments.

Here are three quick ways to build on your momentum and get one step closer to lasting financial freedom.

1. Do something immediately

If you haven't done them already, do those exercises in Part 1. Or schedule some time right now to do them.

You can download the worksheets at KnowYourNumberBonus .com.

2. Listen to my podcast

If you liked this book, then my "Grow it, Don't Blow it" podcast is for you. Each short episode gives actionable advice so you can grow your money wisely and avoid big mistakes.

In fact, you can submit a question you'd like me to answer on the show at www.GrowItPodcast.com.

3. Talk to me

If you're interested in getting help from me directly, let's chat.

"Worst" case, you get answers to your most pressing questions, I give you a few actionable ideas, and you get some clarity on your situation. Best case, we decide to work together and start building your LFF Plan.

Whatever the case, I'll make sure the call is valuable to you and not the dreaded "free consultation" disguised as a sales pitch.

Just email me at bhammer@hammerwealthgroup.com.

NOTES

1. "Cornelius Vanderbilt." *New York Times*. January 5, 1877.
   Web. 5 Jan. 2018. www.query.nytimes.com/mem/archive-free/
   pdf?res=9C01E2D7133AE63BBC4D53DFB766838C669FDE

2. Morningstar Investment Services. *2016 Fundamentals for Investors*.
   Morningstar, 2016. Web. 5 Jan. 2018. www.home.mp.morningstar.com/
   elabsLinks/FundamentalsForInvestors_2016.pdf

3. Morningstar Investment Services. *2016 Fundamentals for Investors*.
   Morningstar, 2016. Web. 5 Jan. 2018. www.home.mp.morningstar.com/
   elabsLinks/FundamentalsForInvestors_2016.pdf

4. Damodaran, Aswath. "S&P Earnings: 1960-Current." NYU, 2017. Web.
   5 Jan. 2018. www.pages.stern.nyu.edu/~adamodar/New_Home_Page/
   datafile/spearn.htm

5. Damodaran, Aswath. "S&P Earnings: 1960–Current." NYU, 2017. Web.
   5 Jan. 2018. www.pages.stern.nyu.edu/~adamodar/New_Home_Page/
   datafile/spearn.htm

6. "$100 in 1975 → 2016 | Inflation Calculator." FinanceRef Inflation
   Calculator, Alioth Finance. Web. 5 Jan. 2018. www.in2013dollars
   .com/1975-dollars-in-2016?amount=100

7. "Compound Annual Growth Rate (Annualized Return)." *Moneychimp*.
   Web. 5 Jan. 2018. www.moneychimp.com/features/market_cagr.htm

8. Laise, Eleanor. "Best Stock Fund of the Decade: CGM Focus." *The Wall
   Street Journal*. 31 Dec. 2009. Web. 5 Jan. 2018. www.wsj.com/articles/
   SB10001424052748704876804574628561609012716?mg=prod/
   accounts-wsj

9. Gawande, Atul. "Personal Best." *The New Yorker*. Oct. 2011. Web. 5 Jan.
   2018. www.newyorker.com/magazine/2011/10/03/personal-best

10. Kitces, Michael. "Why Most Financial Planners Will Soon Be Forced to Lower Their Minimums." *Kitces*. 13 Jan. 2014. Web. 5 Jan. 2018. www.kitces.com/blog/why-most-financial-planners-will-soon-be-forced-to-lower-their-minimums/

11. Ibbotson, Roger G. and Paul D. Kaplan. "Does Asset Allocation Policy Explain 40, 90, or 100 Percent of Performance?" *Financial Analysts Journal*. January/February (2000): 26-33. MangustaRisk. Web. 5 Jan. 2018. www.mangustarisk.com/doc/pdf/Does_Asset_Allocation_Explain_40_90_100_Performance.pdf

12. Arnott, Rob. "Was It Really a Lost Decade?" *Research Affiliates*. Jan. 2010. Web. 5 Jan. 2018. www.researchaffiliates.com/en_us/publications/articles/f_2010_jan_was_it_really_a_lost_decade.html

13. Soe, Aye M. and Ryan Poirier. "SPIVA U.S. Scorecard." *S&P Dow Jones Indices*. 2017. Web. 5 Jan. 2018. www.us.spindices.com/documents/spiva/spiva-us-year-end-2016.pdf

ABOUT BILL

Bill Hammer, Jr. is founder and CEO of Hammer Wealth Group, an independent wealth management firm that helps serious entrepreneurs turn business success into lasting financial freedom.

His clients run and own all kinds of companies—real estate, private equity, professional services, healthcare, staffing, consulting, software, design, franchising, and construction, just to name a few.

Bill's first book, *The 7 Secrets of Extraordinary Investors* (2012), received praise from John C. Bogle, founder of The Vanguard Group, who said, *"This fine compact book explains in simple terms what you need to know to be a successful investor."*

Bill has been quoted in major media outlets like *CNBC, Wall Street Journal, Dow Jones, Fox Business, Chicago Tribune, U.S. News & World Report, Trusts and Estates Magazine, On Wall Street, Financial Advisor Magazine, The Franklin Prosperity Report*, and *Newsday*.

In his previous life, Bill was a conductor who, at age 25, won two Grammy® Awards for his work (Best Classical Album, Best Choral Performance).

Bill lives with his wife (and C.O.O.), Emma, in Princeton, New Jersey, with their dog, Gus.